KNOWIN(

Our Perfect Example

Following God's Ways

Six Studies for Groups or Individuals with Notes for Leaders

Phyllis Bennett

Foreword by J. I. Packer

ZondervanPublishingHouse
Grand Rapids, Michigan

A Division of HarperCollins*Publishers*

OUR PERFECT EXAMPLE: *Following God's Ways*

Requests for information should be addressed to:
Zondervan Publishing House
Grand Rapids, MI 49530

ISBN 0-310-48331-X

Edited by Jack Kuhatschek
Cover design by Mark Veldheer
Cover photograph by Alan Briere, Superstock, Inc.
Interior design by Mark Veldheer & Art Jacobs

Printed in the United States of America

94 95 96 97 98 99 / ❖ DP / 10 9 8 7 6 5 4 3 2 1

Contents

Foreword

One big difference between our current culture and that of a century ago is that the Victorians saw life in terms of roles, while we see it in terms of relationships. Real life, we say, is a matter of relationships, for roles minimize personal involvement while relationships maximize it.

In saying this, we speak more Christian truth than perhaps we realize. For real life according to the Bible means relating not just to other people but also to the personal God who made us. We live and move and exist in him, and it is both scandalous and impoverishing when we ignore him.

Who is he? The startling truth is that he is a *society*. The Father, Son, and Holy Spirit share with each other an intimate and loving relationship. Yet in the unity of their interpersonal life, they constitute a single divine being. God is they, a society and a team, and they are he, the only God there is.

A mystery? An inexplicable reality? Yes, but a life-giving one. It is our privilege not simply to acknowledge the truth of the Trinity but also to enter into a Spirit-sustained relationship with the Father and the Son—a relationship which from one standpoint is *eternal life*, and from another is *knowing God*.

Knowing people involves, first, knowing facts about them and, second, making their acquaintance. How deep our relationship goes depends on how much empathy we have, how many concerns and interests we share, and how much we seek to exalt the one we love. It is the same with knowing God.

The Bible is God's communication to all who hear or read it. Through its varied contents the Triune Lord tells us about himself and calls us to himself. A proper understanding of the Bible will focus at every point on both the information about God and the invitation to know him.

Knowing God Bible Studies are designed to help you achieve this focus. I heartily recommend them. They generate vision, insight, wisdom, and devotion in equal quantities. Use them and you will be blessed.

J. I. Packer

Knowing God Bible Studies

Every Christian desires a deeper, more personal relationship with God. We long to know him better, to feel his presence, and to experience his power in our lives. Jesus himself tells us, "This is eternal life: that they may know you, the only true God, and Jesus Christ, whom you have sent" (John 17:3).

Knowing God Bible Studies can help you build greater intimacy with God. The series explores who God is and how you can know him better. Each guide focuses on a specific attribute of God, such as his love, his faithfulness, or his mercy. The studies are warm and practical and personal—yet they are firmly grounded in Scripture.

The Knowing God series has been field tested in churches across America, representing a wide variety of denominations. This time-intensive process ensures that the guides have solid biblical content, consistent quality, easy-to-use formats, and helpful leader's notes.

Knowing God Bible Studies are designed to be flexible. You can use the guides in any order that is best for you or your group. They are ideal for Sunday-school classes, small groups, one-on-one relationships, or as materials for your quiet times.

Because each guide contains only six studies, you can easily explore more than one attribute of God. In a Sunday-school class, any two guides can be combined for a quarter (twelve weeks), or the entire series can be covered in a year.

Each study deliberately focuses on a limited number of passages, usually only one or two. That allows you to see each passage in its context, avoiding the temptation of prooftexting and the frustration of "Bible hopscotch" (jumping from verse to verse). If you would like to look up additional passages, a Bible concordance will give the most help.

Knowing God Bible Studies help you *discover* what the Bible says rather than simply *telling* you the answers. The questions encourage you to think and to explore options rather than merely to fill in the blanks with one-word answers.

Leader's notes are provided in the back of each guide. They show how to lead a group discussion, provide additional information on questions, and suggest ways to deal with problems that may come up in the discussion. With such helps, someone with little or no experience can lead an effective study.

SUGGESTIONS FOR INDIVIDUAL STUDY

1. Begin each study with prayer. Ask God to help you understand the passage and to apply it to your life.
2. A good modern translation, such as the *New International Version*, the *New American Standard Bible*, or the *New Revised Standard Version*, will give you the most help. Questions in this guide, however, are based on the *New International Version*.
3. Read and reread the passage(s). You must know what the passage says before you can understand what it means and how it applies to you.
4. Write your answers in the space provided in the study guide. This will help you to clearly express your understanding of the passage.

5. Keep a Bible dictionary handy. Use it to look up any unfamiliar words, names, or places.

SUGGESTIONS FOR GROUP STUDY

1. Come to the study prepared. Careful preparation will greatly enrich your time in group discussion.
2. Be willing to join in the discussion. The leader of the group will not be lecturing but will encourage people to discuss what they have learned in the passage. Plan to share what God has taught you in your individual study.
3. Stick to the passage being studied. Base your answers on the verses being discussed rather than on outside authorities such as commentaries or your favorite author or speaker.
4. Try to be sensitive to the other members of the group. Listen attentively when they speak, and be affirming whenever you can. This will encourage more hesitant members of the group to participate.
5. Be careful not to dominate the discussion. By all means participate! But allow others to have equal time.
6. If you are the discussion leader, you will find additional suggestions and helpful ideas in the leader's notes at the back of the guide.

Introducing Our Perfect Example

Hugh Martin, in *The Parables of the Gospels*, tells the story of a rather rough, undignified man who fell in love with a vase in a store window. He proudly bought the vase and placed it on the mantel in his living room. Perched there, it became a judgment on the rest of its surroundings. The drapes looked drab compared to its exquisite exterior. The old chair with the stuffing coming out would no longer do. The wallpaper and the paint needed to be stripped and reapplied. Gradually the whole room was transformed.

That's exactly what happens to us when Jesus, our perfect example, enters our hearts. That which used to appear as a normal and acceptable part of our lifestyle begins to lose its vitality. Old habits are replaced by new ones. What once added color and creativity to the drab routine of life begins to fade in its importance. Previously satisfying forms of entertainment are exchanged for those that will bring glory to Christ. Self-centered relationships are transformed into Christ-centered friendships.

One by one, each piece of life takes on new color and texture until the fabric of our lives has been completely rewoven. As 2 Corinthians 5:17 reminds us, the old is gone, the new has come, because we are new creations in Christ.

This process happens gradually and progressively. It doesn't happen by our reading a list of things we should get rid of and a list of the things we should add to our lives. It happens by our getting to know Jesus as our perfect example. As we fall more deeply in love with him, as the hymn writer says, "The things of earth will grow strangely dim, in the light of His glory and grace." His Spirit working in us does the clean-up job. He lovingly enters the dark places of our lives and fills them with light and beauty.

This study guide is designed to aid you in that process of getting to know God in all of his perfection. Although God is perfect in every way, we will focus on his moral and spiritual perfection—his holiness and purity. We will begin by gazing at the holiness of God as Isaiah portrays it in Isaiah 6. We will then see why God's holiness results in his command, "Be holy because I am holy." Next we'll journey to the New Testament to learn the benefits of fixing our eyes on Jesus, allowing him to discipline us for our good, that we might share in his holiness.

Our last three studies will challenge us to live a life of purity. Jesus himself demonstrates for us that purity of heart leads to loving servanthood. We will also learn what to do when our life's course of purity is interrupted by strong temptation.

As you go through this study guide, ask the Holy Spirit to strip away anything in your life that is less than pure or holy. Don't be afraid of the stripping process. Just focus on loving him, and he will graciously and gently make you more like Jesus, our perfect example.

Phyllis Bennett

1

"Holy, Holy, Holy"

Isaiah 6

Early in his career, Johann Dannecker, a 19th-century sculptor, became well-known for his statues of Greek goddesses. As he was approaching his prime of life, he decided to devote himself to the creation of a masterpiece. And so he chose to carve a figure of Christ.

After two false starts, he finally created a statue of Christ that was so flawless and exquisitely beautiful that when people gazed upon it, it led them to worship and adore Jesus himself. Later, Napoleon wrote to him and said, "Come to Paris, and make for me a statue of Venus for the Louvre." But no offer could tempt the heart of Dannecker. His reply was one of absolute devotion. He said, "Sir, the hands that carved the Christ can never again carve a heathen goddess." Apparently Dannecker's experience of sculpting Christ had so purified his heart that he could not be tempted to go back to his old ways, even for financial gain.

Purity is a state of the heart where there is complete devotion to God. There are no conflicting loyalties, no mixed motives, no divided interests, and no hypocrisy. Or as Søren Kierkegaard once said, "Purity of heart is to will one thing." In Isaiah 6 we will relive Isaiah's encounter in the temple with the God of absolute purity.

1. What historical or contemporary person best exemplifies for you the quality of purity?

2. Read Isaiah 6:1–8. In the year that King Uzziah died, Isaiah saw a vision of the Lord (vv. 1–4). What do the details of that vision reveal about the Lord's character?

3. How did Isaiah respond to what he saw and heard (v. 5)?

Why did he respond in this way?

4. Have you ever had a similar response to the presence of the Lord? Explain.

5. Isaiah confessed his sin and the sin of his people as that of "unclean lips." In what ways might our lips be used for unclean purposes?

6. "Coals of fire were taken inside the Most Holy Place on the Day of Atonement (Lev. 16:12), when sacrifice was made to atone for sin."[1] How does this help to explain the seraph's actions in verses 6–7?

7. In verse 8 the Lord finally speaks. Why do you suppose he didn't speak earlier?

8. In a similar vein, what might prevent or hinder the Lord from speaking to us about his plans for our lives?

9. What was to be the essence of Isaiah's message to the people (vv. 9–13)?

How would you feel if you were chosen to deliver such a message? Explain.

10. How might Isaiah have been tempted to distort the message if he hadn't first seen God in all his purity and holiness?

11. When have you found it difficult to deliver God's message to others and not give in to being a people pleaser? (Consider family members, friends, business associates, and so on.)

12. Who in your life needs to be reminded of God's holiness and his desire for us to live a holy life?

What impact might such a message have on that person's life?

13. Ask God to touch your life and lips with his holiness, so that you might be a clean channel and messenger to others in his timing.

Memory Verse

I am a man of unclean lips, and I live among a people of unclean lips, and my eyes have seen the King, the LORD Almighty.

Isaiah 6:5

BETWEEN STUDIES

Keep a diary each day this week of how you use your lips for holy or unholy purposes. Thank the Lord daily for ways he has displayed his holiness to you and spoken through you to others. Ask his forgiveness for times you have allowed your lips to speak less than holy words.

Sing a hymn about the holiness of God each day after your time of prayer.

Holy, Holy, Holy Lord God Almighty,
Early in the morning our song shall rise to Thee.
Holy, Holy, Holy there is none beside Thee,
God in three persons, blessed Trinity.

Note

1. *The NIV Study Bible* (Grand Rapids, Mich.: Zondervan, 1985), p. 1026.

2

"Be Holy, Because I Am Holy"

Leviticus 19

When was the last time you received a letter that was signed "Sincerely yours"? Often we use words without really understanding their meaning or their origin. *Sincerely* was originally used by ancient sculptors to mark a flawless masterpiece. It meant "without wax" (*sin* = "without"; *cera* = "wax") because wax was commonly used by sculptors to hide defects or to patch a chipped nose or a poorly shaped finger. By that definition, God's signature can always be written "Sincerely yours" or "without wax or defect."

In Leviticus 19 God commands his people to be "Sincerely his," to be holy as he is holy. His process of purification included giving them a list of rules designed to keep them from becoming involved in anything unholy.

As you study this chapter, allow these Old Testament laws to sift out any unholy ways in your life that might keep you from being free to sign any letter of your life as "Sincerely his."

1. What rules can you remember from your growing up at home that were laid down for your moral protection?

Give examples of how you benefited from one or two of these rules.

2. Read Leviticus 19. Why is the Lord's holiness the ultimate reason and motivation for our being holy (vv. 1–2)?

3. What do the following verses reveal about the ways holiness should have affected Israel's relationship with God?

❑ verse 4:

❑ verses 5–8:

❑ verse 12:

❑ verse 30:

What implications can you draw from each command for your relationship with God today?

4. How might God's holiness have been violated if each of the following vocational commands had not been obeyed?

❑ verses 9–10:

✗ ❑ verse 13b:

❏ verse 19:

❏ verses 23–25:

❏ verses 35–36:

Which of these commands still apply today as we carry out the vocational mandate God gave us in Genesis 1:28?

How could or how has our society applied them?

5. Why do you suppose the following commands about personal defilement were so important to God?

❏ verse 26:

❑ verse 27:

❑ verse 28:

❑ verse 31:

Which of these commands about personal defilement still hold true for us today? Explain.

6. The last set of commands have to do with how we treat others. How were the Israelites to demonstrate holiness when relating to the following groups?

❑ their neighbors (vv. 11, 13, 16–18):

❑ those who were "different" or less fortunate (vv. 13–15, 20–22, 33):

How should these commands affect the way we relate to those around us?

7. As you examine your life in light of the categories in Leviticus 19, where do you sense the Spirit pricking your conscience to demonstrate greater holiness because your Lord is holy?

8. What is one step you could take this week to instill holiness in this area of your life?

Memory Verse

Be holy because I, the LORD your God, am holy.

Leviticus 19:2

BETWEEN STUDIES

Clip out of the newspaper or circle this week any articles that speak of our society's awareness of the blind, lame, poor, or those unjustly treated. Pray that God's love would be real to the people represented by these articles through the Christians they encounter.

3

Fixing Our Eyes On Jesus

Hebrews 12:1-13

On your mark!
Get set! Go!"

Any runner in the starting blocks knows that one of the most deadly mistakes of a competitor is losing one's focus. That was Zola Budd's testimony after running against Mary Decker in the 3000 meter finals of the 1984 Olympics. Zola was a promising South African teenage runner who kept a poster of her idol, Mary Decker, on the wall beside her bed. Never did she dream she would someday run against Mary in the Olympics. But in the final heat of the '84 Olympics, they met each other face to face. At about the 1700-meter mark, Decker hit one of Budd's legs, throwing Budd off balance just a bit. Five strides later, they bumped again, causing Budd to land awkwardly. As a result, Decker tripped on Budd's leg which was thrown out to the side as Budd tried to regain her balance. Then Budd looked back to see her idol falling to the ground.

It was that glance backwards that caused Zola Budd to lose her focus and her determination to win. Unfortunately, after years of training and endless hours of discipline, it is often only that inquisitive look that makes the difference between receiving a gold or a silver or a bronze medal.

How important is your focus in life? What effect does it have on your ability to run life's race? Climb into the starting blocks, steady your shaky knees, and fix your eyes on Jesus as you study this passage. The race is winnable with him as your focus!

---

1. Name one task you enjoy doing with complete concentration and one in which you tend to get easily distracted.

2. Read Hebrews 12:1–13. According to verse 1, as we run the race of life a "great cloud of witnesses" is watching and cheering us on. Who are some of these witnesses (see Heb. 11)?

How do the lives of these saints encourage you to keep on running?

3. As we run the race, what does the author of Hebrews encourage us to do (vv. 1–2)?

4. If we are to throw off everything that hinders *and* the sin that so easily entangles, we can assume that sin and hindrances are two different categories.

What sins might entangle a Christian as they run the race? What hindrances other than sin might entangle us? (Give several examples of each.)

Sins	Hindrances

In each category, pick one which most often slows you down in your race. How can you throw them off like you would bulky pieces of clothing?

5. How would you describe in your own words the One on whom our eyes are to be fixed (vv. 2–4)?

6. When the Lord disciplines us, what are two extreme reactions we are cautioned *not* to take (v. 5)?

Which tends to be your reaction to the disciplining hand of God? Explain.

7. Why does God discipline us (vv. 5–11)?

8. How is God's discipline similar to and different from the way a father disciplines his children (vv. 9–10)?

9. According to the author, how do the short-term aspects of God's discipline compare to the long-term benefits (v. 11)?

10. How have you experienced the Lord's discipline recently?

11. In what ways have you seen the Lord's discipline produce in you "a harvest of righteousness and peace"?

12. How does the author of Hebrews encourage us to cooperate with God's discipline, and why (vv. 12–13)?

13. In your life right now, where are you experiencing a lame limb, a "weak knee," or a "feeble arm"? (Perhaps your "weak knee" is a fear you need to commit to Jesus, a nagging bad habit, a broken relationship, a neglected prayer life, and so on.)

14. Pray and ask God to help you "fix your eyes on Jesus" as you turn over this area of discipline to him.

Memory Verse

Let us run with perseverance the race marked out for us. Let us fix our eyes on Jesus, the author and perfecter of our faith, who for the joy set before him endured the cross, scorning its shame, and sat down at the right hand of the throne of God.

Hebrews 12:1–2

BETWEEN STUDIES

Focus on one area of your life this week that needs the Lord's discipline. Perhaps it's an area where you lack self-control, such as your diet, your spending habits, your thought life, or your time alone with God. Perhaps you need to rethink your daily priorities in light of the Lord's values.

Whatever the area, ask the Lord to help you cooperate with his discipline to this particular area of your life. What can you do this week to "strengthen your feeble arms and weak knees"? How can you "make level paths for your feet"? (Be specific.)

Throughout the week, make sure you fix your eyes on Jesus, the author and perfecter of your faith.

4

Following Christ's Example

John 13:1-17

When Dr. Henry Ironside, a great twentieth-century Bible expositor, was a young boy he helped his widowed mother by working during his vacations, apprenticing himself to a cobbler. It was his job to pound leather for shoe soles. He would take pieces of cowhide, soaked in water, and pound them until they were hard and dry. It was a difficult job, and after endless pounding he would get very tired.

One day he noticed that an ungodly cobbler who worked down the street was not pounding. Instead, he would nail the soles while still wet. When asked why, he responded, "So they will come back quicker." But the Christian owner for whom Henry worked explained to him, "I do not cobble just for 50¢ or 75¢. I do it for the glory of God. In heaven, I expect every shoe returned to me in a pile, and I do not want the Lord to say, "Dan, that was a poor job. You did not do your best."

In John 13, Jesus shows us how even the smallest task can be done for the glory of God and the benefit of others.

1. Describe a recent situation in which someone was a servant to you.

What surprised you the most about their servanthood?

2. Read John 13:1–17. According to verses 1–3, what did Jesus know about his past, present, and future?

3. In light of this knowledge, why is it surprising what Jesus does next (vv. 4–5)?

How do Jesus' actions contrast with the way powerful people often treat others?

4. In verses 6–11 Peter and Jesus enter into a debate. Why do you think Peter objects to having his feet washed by Jesus?

5. What does Peter fail to realize about Jesus' actions and what they symbolize?

6. Although we only need a "bath" from Jesus once, in what sense do we need him to wash our feet each day (vv. 8, 10)?

7. After washing his disciples' feet, how does Jesus explain the reasons for what he did (vv. 12–17)?

8. Some groups take Jesus' words in verse 14 literally and hold feet-washing services. Yet what are some other specific ways we can serve each other?

9. How has the Lord used you as a "servant" to others recently?

How were you "blessed" by serving them (v. 17)?

10. Christ calls us to follow his perfect example of love by serving each other. What is one way you can serve a fellow believer this week?

Pray and ask the Lord for wisdom and a servant's heart in following through with your desire.

Memory Verse

Now that I, your Lord and Teacher, have washed your feet, you also should wash one another's feet.

John 13:14

BETWEEN STUDIES

Keep a running list this week of times when others ask you to serve and times when you offer to serve others without being asked. At the end of the week, try to determine what you have learned about your capacity for servanthood.

Asked to Serve	Served Without Being Asked	What I Learned

5

Purity in Action

Genesis 39

It has often been said, "It is not enough for a gardener to love flowers; he must also hate weeds." In following Christ's example of perfection, we too must not just love the pure lifestyle to which he calls us. We must also hate those things that can interrupt that purity.

It is difficult to maintain moral purity in a country where the divorce rate has more than quadrupled since 1960 and where one out of every 250 people is HIV positive. Yet a study of Joseph's life can teach us not only how to love the flowers of purity but also how to hate the weeds of immorality.

1. When have you been tempted to compromise your standards due to peer pressure or a temptation of the flesh?

2. Read Genesis 39. How does Joseph demonstrate unadulterated devotion to the Lord, and how is it rewarded (vv. 1–6)?

3. Perhaps we can gain some insight into Joseph's character by answering the following question: To which of your friends would you be willing to entrust everything you own?

What is it about their character that would allow you to trust them that deeply?

4. Joseph continues to demonstrate his firm devotion to God under difficult circumstances. What reasons does he give for refusing to sleep with Potiphar's wife (vv. 7–9)?

5. How might a person's position in life give rise to opportunities and/or temptations to use the power of his position for personal gain? (Give examples of this kind of abuse of power from the business world, family life, church and/or community involvements.)

6. The "wicked thing" (v. 9) would have been a sin against Potiphar and his wife as well. Why do you feel Joseph only said it would be a sin against God?

7. What practical lessons can we learn from Joseph's actions about how to handle persistent temptations (vv. 10–12; see also 2 Tim. 2:22)?

8. How could one of Joseph's actions have helped you handle a recent temptation?

9. Purity of character is not always rewarded with respect. What manipulative steps does Potiphar's wife take to try to destroy Joseph's reputation (vv. 13–19)?

10. When has your attempt to resist temptation been confronted with lack of respect, misunderstanding, or criticism?

How did you handle the situation?

11. How does the strength of Joseph's character surface and get rewarded once again (vv. 20–23)?

12. Proverbs 4:23 gives wise counsel to those who want to resist temptation: "Guard your heart, it is the wellspring of life." In what area of your life are you facing persistent temptation?

What one step could you take this week to "guard your heart" against temptation in this area?

Memory Verse

Flee the evil desires of youth, and pursue righteousness, faith, love and peace, along with those who call on the Lord out of a pure heart.

2 Timothy 2:22

BETWEEN STUDIES

Sins of the flesh are great temptations for all of us. Initiate a conversation with a Christian brother or sister this week whom you know has overcome a past addiction to alcohol, sex, drugs, food, or something similar. Ask the person what helped him or her bring this area under the control of the Spirit. Make a list of principles the person has applied in overcoming temptation that you could implement in your life. For each principle you list, see if you can give that principle a scriptural basis to deepen your sense of conviction in applying it to your life.

6

Taking Up Our Cross

Mark 8:31–9:1

John Wesley once said, "Give me a hundred men who fear nothing but sin, and desire nothing but God and I will shake the world. I care not a straw whether they be clergymen or laymen; and such alone will overthrow the kingdom of Satan and build up the Kingdom of God on earth."

Jesus desires intense dedication from his followers. He calls us to deny ourselves, take up our cross, and follow him wholeheartedly. But in Mark 8:31–9:1 we discover that he only asks us to do what he was willing to do himself.

1. Describe a time when someone rebuked you strongly, and at first you didn't respond well, but later you saw the wisdom behind their words.

2. Read Mark 8:31–33. Notice the strong verbs Jesus uses in describing what will happen to him soon. Why do you suppose he relates each of these specifics to his disciples?

3. Why do you think Peter responds to Jesus' statements by rebuking him privately?

4. Why does Jesus severely rebuke Peter in front of all the other disciples (v. 33)?

5. Jesus not only rebukes Peter but refers to him as "Satan" (v. 33). How was Peter tempting Jesus in the same way Satan did in Matthew 4:8–10?

6. How can we know whether we are motivated by the things of God or the things of men?

7. Read Mark 8:34–9:1. We know that children learn best in what are often called "teachable moments." Why was this particular situation a "teachable moment" for what Jesus teaches next?

8. Describe a "teachable moment" you have had with one of your children or with a friend.

9. What does it mean to you to deny yourself, take up your cross, and follow Jesus (v. 34)?

10. If we choose *not* to follow Jesus and decide to pursue our own goals instead, what will be the short-term and long-term consequences (vv. 35–38)?

What does Jesus say will be the short-term and long-term consequences if we choose to follow him (8:35–9:1)?

11. How do these consequences encourage you to follow Jesus whatever the costs?

12. Describe a time in your life recently when you "denied yourself" and took up your cross.

13. Think about the coming week. In what specific area do you sense God asking you to deny yourself, take up your cross, and follow him?

Pray and ask the Lord for strength to follow through on this commitment.

Memory Verse

If anyone would come after me, he must deny himself and take up his cross and follow me. For whoever wants to save his life will lose it, but whoever loses his life for me and for the gospel will save it.

Mark 8:34–35

BETWEEN STUDIES

Take some time this week to examine your primary goals in life and the amount of time you spend pursuing those goals. Are you building your own little kingdom by putting yourself first and seeking to make your life as prosperous, comfortable, and carefree as possible? Or are you helping to build Christ's kingdom by putting him first and serving others in sacrificial love?

Jim Elliot, a young missionary who was killed while trying to reach the Auca Indians with the gospel, once wrote: "He is no fool who gives that which he cannot keep to gain that which he cannot lose." Ask God for grace to live wisely in light of Christ's coming.

Leader's Notes

Leading a Bible discussion—especially for the first time—can make you feel both nervous and excited. If you are nervous, realize that you are in good company. Many biblical leaders, such as Moses, Joshua, and the apostle Paul, felt nervous and inadequate to lead others (see, for example, 1 Cor. 2:3). Yet God's grace was sufficient for them, just as it will be for you.

Some excitement is also natural. Your leadership is a gift to the others in the group. Keep in mind, however, that other group members also share responsibility for the group. Your role is simply to stimulate discussion by asking questions and encouraging people to respond. The suggestions listed below can help you to be an effective leader.

PREPARING TO LEAD

1. Ask God to help you understand and apply the passage to your own life. Unless that happens, you will not be prepared to lead others.
2. Carefully work through each question in the study guide. Meditate and reflect on the passage as you formulate your answers.
3. Familiarize yourself with the leader's notes for the study. These will help you understand the purpose of the study

and will provide valuable information about the questions in the study.

4. Pray for the various members of the group. Ask God to use these studies to make you better disciples of Jesus Christ.
5. Before the first meeting, make sure each person has a study guide. Encourage them to prepare beforehand for each study.

LEADING THE STUDY

1. Begin the study on time. If people realize that the study begins on schedule, they will work harder to arrive on time.
2. At the beginning of your first time together, explain that these studies are designed to be discussions, not lectures. Encourage everyone to participate, but realize that some may be hesitant to speak during the first few sessions.
3. Read the introductory paragraph at the beginning of the discussion. This will orient the group to the passage being studied.
4. Read the passage aloud. You may choose to do this yourself, or you might ask for volunteers.
5. The questions in the guide are designed to be used just as they are written. If you wish, you may simply read each one aloud to the group. Or you may prefer to express them in your own words. Unnecessary rewording of the questions, however, is not recommended.
6. Don't be afraid of silence. People in the group may need time to think before responding.
7. Avoid answering your own questions. If necessary, rephrase a question until it is clearly understood. Even an eager group will quickly become passive and silent if they think the leader will do most of the talking.
8. Encourage more than one answer to each question. Ask, "What do the rest of you think?" or "Anyone else?" until several people have had a chance to respond.

9. Try to be affirming whenever possible. Let people know you appreciate their insights into the passage.
10. Never reject an answer. If it is clearly wrong, ask, "Which verse led you to that conclusion?" Or let the group handle the problem by asking them what they think about the question.
11. Avoid going off on tangents. If people wander off course, gently bring them back to the passage being considered.
12. Conclude your time together with conversational prayer. Ask God to help you apply those things that you learned in the study.
13. End on time. This will be easier if you control the pace of the discussion by not spending too much time on some questions or too little on others.

Many more suggestions and helps are found in the book *Leading Bible Discussions* (InterVarsity Press). Reading it would be well worth your time.

STUDY ONE

"Holy, Holy, Holy"

ISAIAH 6

Purpose: To discover that before we can speak God's message to others we must realize his holiness and purity.

Question 1 Every study begins with a "warm-up question," which is discussed *before* reading the passage. A warm-up question is designed to do three things:

First, it helps to break the ice. Because a warm-up question doesn't require any knowledge of the passage or any special preparation, it can get people talking and can help them to feel more comfortable with each other.

Second, a warm-up question can motivate people to study the passage at hand. At the beginning of the study, people in the group aren't necessarily ready to jump into the world of the Bible. Their minds may be on other things (their kids, a problem at work, an upcoming meeting) that have nothing to do with the study. A warm-up question can capture their interest and draw them into the discussion by raising important issues related to the study. The question becomes a bridge between their personal lives and the answers found in Scripture.

Third, a good warm-up question can reveal where people's thoughts or feelings need to be transformed by Scripture. That is why it is important to ask the warm-up question *before* reading the passage. The passage might inhibit the spontaneous, honest answers people might have given, because they feel compelled to give biblical answers. The warm-up question allows them to compare their personal thoughts and feelings with what they later discover in Scripture.

Question 2 Isaiah mentions that above the Lord were "seraphs" (v. 2). *The NIV Study Bible* gives the following definition of these unusual beings: "*Seraphs*—Angelic beings not mentioned elsewhere. The Hebrew root underlying this word means 'burn,' perhaps to indicate their purity as God's ministers. They correspond to the 'living creatures' of Rev. 4:6–9, each of whom also had six wings" (*The NIV Study Bible* [Grand Rapids, Mich.: Zondervan, 1985], p. 1025).

"*Covered their faces*—Apparently they could not gaze directly at the glory of God" (*The NIV Study Bible*, p. 1025).

"The Lord was seated upon a throne, high and lifted up, and so very high. As judges and kings sat upon their thrones, so the Lord is sitting upon His. He is thus seen as One who is already king, engaged in the act of judgment. The long, loose, flowing robes or skirts of the robe were filling the palace, so that there was no room left for anyone to stand. It is a scene of glorious majesty. As the vision is seen by Isaiah, he is silent, and his silence simply focuses attention upon the unspeakable exaltation of the Lord. Isaiah is to be called to a ministry in which the sovereign power of God will be displayed, and in which judgment is to be prominent. In preparation for such a ministry there must be a vision of God's holiness. Indeed, the entire scene befits the solemnity of the message. Our attention is directed immediately to the Lord as Him who alone is sovereign, who can both create and destroy, and in whose hands are the times of all men and nations" (Edward J. Young, *The Book of Isaiah, Vol. 1, Ch.1–18* [Grand Rapids, Mich.: Eerdmans, 1981], p. 238).

Question 5 Encourage your group to think of ways that our lips can be used for unclean purposes—gossiping, bragging, taking the glory when it belongs to God, telling lies, tearing down another's self-confidence and reputation, arguing, blaming, tattling, and so on.

Question 6 "In a symbolical sense fire is regarded as having purifying power. The application of fire to the lips, therefore, symbolized the fact that those lips were cleansed. This cleansing, however, is not the work of fire, but of the Lord; it rests upon the fact, as is brought out in the next verse, that a sacrifice for sin has been offered. Consequently, this passage is not simply another illustration of the ancient belief that fire was regarded as possessing purifying power" (Young, p. 250).

Question 7 There are several possible answers to this question:

a) Our holy God will not speak to sinful humanity until sin is confessed and cleansed.

b) Sinners are not prepared to hear God speak until sin is confessed, so why should God speak in such instances?

c) Isaiah might have responded improperly to God's call without confessing his sin first.

Question 9 "How often God had commanded the world to hear his word. In this hearing, which is enjoined upon all people, there is included an understanding and a willingness. Isaiah's ministry, however, is to counteract this command. He is to preach so that men cannot do what they have been commanded to do. And yet, the responsibility and guilt lie upon the nation. . . . Isaiah's ministry was to preach to stony soil, so that it might be apparent that the people were no longer the theocracy, and that they were rightfully ripe for banishment from their land. God's work of hardening therefore attests the fact that the time for the banishment from Palestine was at hand" (Young, p. 258–59).

Question 12 Use this question to begin your time of prayer together as a group.

STUDY TWO

"Be Holy, Because I Am Holy"

LEVITICUS 19

Purpose: To realize that the Lord's holiness is the ultimate reason and motivation for our being holy.

Question 1 Be sensitive to the fact that each group member has grown up in a different type of home, some with strict rules, and others that were lacking in discipline. Try to focus the discussion on positive rules established by parents for wise protection of the children in either type of home.

Question 2 "Holiness is the key theme of Leviticus, ringing like a refrain in various forms throughout the book (e.g., v. 45; 19:2; 20:7, 26; 21:8, 15; 22:9, 16, 32). The word 'holy' appears more often in Leviticus than in any other book of the Bible. Israel was to be totally consecrated to God. Her holiness was to be expressed in every aspect of her life, to the extent that all of life had a certain ceremonial quality. Because of who God is and what he has done (11:45), his people must dedicate themselves fully to him" (*The NIV Study Bible*, p. 160).

Questions 3b, 4b, 5b, 6b In answering these questions, remember that Christ came to fulfill the law, not to abolish it. Though we are not held accountable to do everything today that the law required, there are some basic principles underlying many of these Old Testament laws that can help us today to enrich our relationship with God and others. These questions are geared to help the group grapple with these underlying principles, not to get entangled in the legalism of the laws themselves.

Question 4 The term "vocational commands" refers to commands that God gave us to be his people in our vocations or our life work.

Verse 9: "The harvest was to be used for the work of mercy that formed a part of the Israelite's obligation to his neighbor, and the poor as well as aliens were therefore allowed to eat what had previously been intended for the field spirits. In this manner, the practice of mercy was to become one of Israel's virtues. It was entirely consistent with this for the rabbis to say that a person actually was duty bound to thank a beggar, since he had given him the opportunity to show mercy"

(A. Noordtzij, *Leviticus*, Bible Student's Commentary [Grand Rapids, Mich.: Zondervan, 1982], pp. 195–96).

Perhaps today God wouldn't hold us accountable not to reap the edges of our fields for the sake of the poor (v. 9), but the principle still holds true. We are to manage what God has given us in such a way that we are aware of those who are poor and less fortunate than we are, and give part of what we earn to them. This can be done through a financial gift, through passing on old clothes or items of furniture, and in many other ways. Help your group brain-storm other possibilities.

In our society today it pleases the Lord when we pay people promptly for work they have done for us (v. 13). This principle also has implications for bill paying, paying employees, paying taxes, and so on.

Verse 23: "The fruit is taboo for three years, just as religiously the uncircumcised male is taboo. Possibly the original reason was that the fruit belonged to the spirit of the land (the baal), just as all increase of every kind is always regarded as belonging to God. In any case, it is a sound agricultural principle; it gives the tree time to make wood and ultimately bear better crops" (N. H. Snaith, *Leviticus*, New Century Bible [Greenwood, South Carolina: The Attic Press, Inc., 1967], p. 133).

Question 5 Verse 26: "The blood shed in the sacrifices was sacred. It epitomized the life of the sacrificial victim. Since life was sacred, blood (a symbol of life) had to be treated with respect. Eating blood was therefore strictly forbidden" (*The NIV Study Bible*, p. 168).

Verse 28: "Just as slaves were marked as their master's property by having a sign put on them, worshipers of certain gods had the custom of inscribing such a token on some portion of their bodies. The custom was no doubt explicitly forbidden in the present verse because at that time it still retained a strong Canaanite character. Tattooing was common in later Judaism, but its pagan tendencies had by then disappeared" (A. Noordtzij, *Leviticus*, pp. 258–59).

Verse 31: "The following regulation forbids the Israelites from making inquiries of 'mediums' or 'spiritists.' The entire ancient Near Eastern world, and the Greeks and Romans as well, believed that the passage of deceased persons into the visible world gave them access to increased knowledge and that it was possible for the living, especially women (I Samuel 28:3), to compel them to disclose this knowledge by means of various occult practices. Such a spirit of the dead could enter into either a man or woman (Lev. 20:27), and the latter thereby became a 'medium' who could exercise control over the spirit. The term that is rendered 'seek out' here implies a request for advice and assistance, and this is the only place where it is used in relation to spirits of the dead. In all other instances it indicates a turning to the Lord. To seek out such spirits resulted in uncleanness, i.e., exclusion from the Lord's worship with its demand for purity" (A. Noordtzij, *Leviticus*, pp. 206–7).

Questions 7–8 Encourage the group to pick just one category on which to focus. We all need to take baby steps in order to see progress as we grow in Christ. Try to steer the group away from being so overwhelmed with their lack of holiness that they can't see the Lord empowering them for one step at a time.

STUDY THREE

Fixing Our Eyes On Jesus

HEBREWS 12:1–13

Purpose: To learn the importance of fixing our eyes on Jesus as we run our spiritual race and to cooperate with our heavenly Father when he disciplines us.

Question 2 This question can be threatening to those who don't know a lot about the Old Testament. It can, however, stimulate excellent discussion about the Old Testament saints who have modeled for us how to walk by faith. This question is given to put Hebrews 12:1 in its proper context following the great cloud of witnesses in Hebrews 11.

"*Surrounded by such a great cloud of witnesses*. The imagery suggests an athletic contest in a great amphitheater. The witnesses are the heroes of the past who have just been mentioned (ch. 11). They are not spectators but inspiring examples. The Greek work translated 'witnesses' is the origin of the English word 'martyr' and means 'testifiers, witnesses.' They bear testimony to the power of faith and to God's faithfulness" (*The NIV Study Bible*, p. 1874).

Question 4 It will be less threatening to the group if you look first at broad categories of sin and hindrances in their lives. Then narrow down to more specific areas of sin and hindrances. This question can generate a lot of personal sharing.

Question 5 "*Perfecter of our faith.* Our faith, which has its beginning in him, is also complete in him; he is both the start and the end of the race. He is also the supreme witness who has already run the race and overcome" (*The NIV Study Bible*, p. 1874).

Question 6 "*Punishes*—The Greek for this verb means 'to whip.' God chastens us in order to correct our faults" (*The NIV Study Bible*, p. 1874).

Question 7 Often the question is asked, "Do we experience the anger or wrath of God in the New Testament in the way that people did in the Old Testament?" The answer is no, in that all of God's wrath was poured out on Christ on the cross. Romans 8:1 tells us, "Therefore, there is now no condemnation for those who are in Christ Jesus." Although we do not experience his wrath, we do experience his discipline, because he loves us as his children.

Verses 5–6: "*Paideias, chastening,* in the classical Greek means 'instruction,' 'education.' But in biblical Greek the instruction and education are given by means of correction through the severe discipline of God. The aim of such discipline remains the same but its use varies, for it is put in operation to deliver from sin, to perfect in holiness, or to establish in the faith; here it is administered to promote endurance. The readers are urged, therefore, not to despise or regard lightly such discipline as if God were not behind it, or to drift into despondency, for God never tries anyone beyond his strength. God's strong affection for the children *whom he receives*, or adopts, does not overrule His purpose for them, which is spiritual development to a fuller life of righteousness. He cannot, therefore, overlook those faults or misdemeanors which mar their spiritual growth." (Thomas Hewitt, *The Epistle to the Hebrews*, [Grand Rapids, Mich.: Eerdmans, 1978], p. 193)

Questions 13–14 Consider, for example, a fear you need to commit to Jesus, a nagging bad habit, a broken relationship, a neglected prayer life, or an unorganized area of your life.

STUDY FOUR

Following Christ's Example

JOHN 13:1–17

Purpose: To learn from Jesus' example how even the smallest task can be done for the glory of God and the benefit of others.

Question 2 "Our Lord was acutely aware of all the details concerning the next twenty-four hours. Here he manifests His sovereignty and his omniscience. Jesus knew *where* he was from. He knew he had come from God. He knew *where* he was going. He knew he should depart out of this world. He knew *when* he was going. He knew that his hour had come. He knew to *whom* he was going. He knew he was going to the Father.

"He knew *why* he had come and *why* He was going. He knew the Father had given all things into His hands. He knew that the Father had such confidence in Him that he would finish the purpose for which he came" (John Mitchell, *An Everlasting Love, A Devotional study of the Gospel of John* [Portland, Oregon: Multnomah Press, 1982], p. 249).

Question 3 When we are secure in who we are—as Jesus was—we can be free to serve others without embarrassment or inhibitions.

"Here we have love displayed in meekness and service. Did you ever think of the distance the Lord traveled? He left the glory, took His place in the human race, and was rejected and despised of men. He revealed Himself in His glory and power to the people of His day. And here I find Him on His knees washing the dirty feet of His disciples. What a sight for the angels! What a distance He traveled from the glory to the place of a slave.

"Here is One before whom angels fall in worship, adoration, and praise. And if they could gaze out of the battlements of heaven and look down upon earth, they would see the Savior on His knees with a basin of water, not only washing feet, but taking a towel and wiping them. I say, what an example." (John Mitchell, *An Everlasting Love*, p. 250).

Question 6 "*Only to wash his feet*—A man would bathe himself before going to a feast. When he arrived, he only needed to wash his feet to be entirely clean again" (*The NIV Study Bible*, p. 1623).

Question 7 "*Teacher . . . Lord.* An instructor would normally be called 'Teacher,' but 'Lord' referred to one occupying the supreme place. Jesus accepted both titles" (*The NIV Study Bible*, p. 1623).

Question 9 There are many ways we can serve others. Try to direct the conversation away from a vague list of possible acts of servanthood to one specific act the Holy Spirit could inspire each group member to carry out this week. Each group member will probably go home with a different way to serve someone.

STUDY FIVE

Purity in Action

GENESIS 39

Purpose: To understand that God calls us not only to love what is pure but also to hate and avoid what is evil.

Question 1 You might suggest that the answers to this question could come from childhood or teenage experiences rather than recent adult experiences. When we share from our past, it's often less threatening.

Question 3 There may be some group members who don't feel they know anyone to whom they could entrust everything they own. Give them permission to give "no one" as their answer. Perhaps they could describe a person they feel they could trust with *some* of what they own.

Question 7 "The garment that Joseph had to leave in the woman's hands was actually the undergarment, a long shirt tied about the hips. It was not the coatlike cape, which one was not accustomed to wear indoors. This means that Joseph fled completely undressed, at once disgracefully and honorable. 'Out of the house' need not mean onto the street; the living quarters of an ancient Oriental house surrounded a courtyard" (Gerhard Von Rad, *Genesis*, The Old Testament Library [Philadelphia, Penna.: The Westminster Press, 1952], p. 361).

This question should stimulate good discussion of how to handle temptation. Possible answers may include:

Remove yourself immediately from the temptation.

With “day after day” temptations, strong consistent refusals, as Joseph gave, are a must. We must not only refuse to do what is being asked but also refuse even to remain in the situation (v. 10).

State to the person posing the temptation that the reason why you can’t give in to the temptation is that it would be a sin against God.

Question 9 “The sudden change from sexual desire to the hate in which the woman acts with great presence of mind is realistically described also in II Sam. 13:15. The narrators of these literary epochs know a great deal about the depths of the human psyche. The woman's situation was critical because of Joseph's refusal and flight. She saves herself by using the abandoned garment as evidence against Joseph and by making witnesses of the men of the house” (Gerhard Von Rad, *Genesis*, p. 361).

Question 11 “*The place where the king’s prisoner’s were confined.* Though understandably angry (see v. 19), Potiphar put Joseph in the ‘house of the captain of the guard’ (40:3)—certainly not the worst prison available” (*The NIV Study Bible*, p. 66).

STUDY SIX

Taking Up Our Cross

MARK 8:31–9:1

Purpose: To realize why it is essential to deny ourselves, take up our cross, and follow Jesus.

Question 2 “‘Peter took him aside,’ may mean literally that Peter ‘drew him to him,’ with a gesture implying protection, if not superiority” (Vincent Taylor, *The Gospel According to Mark*, [New York: St. Martin's Press, 1966], p. 379).

Question 4 Although Peter took Jesus aside privately, perhaps the rebuke was overheard by the disciples. Jesus must have felt that a public rebuke was necessary so that all the disciples would know of Jesus’ displeasure with Peter’s suggestion. If he had rebuked Peter privately, there would still have been confusion in the minds of the disciples.

Public rebuke is necessary when the rebuke brings clarity to those who have heard the statement that needs to be corrected.

"Peter's interposition implies the same kind of temptation which presented itself in the wilderness, that of accepting the popularly expected Messianic role." (Vincent Taylor, *The Gospel According to Mark*, p. 380).

Question 5 For other scriptural support to help understand why Jesus called Peter "Satan," look up the following verses:

- ❑ Luke 22:3
- ❑ John 13:27
- ❑ Acts 5:3
- ❑ James 3:13–15

Question 6 This may be a hard question for some. If we are not walking in step with the Spirit (Gal. 5:25), then we can be Satan's tool to dispense wisdom that is not from above (James 3:13–15), that is earthly, spiritual, and of the Devil. It may not be our desire or our intent, but it can still happen.

Question 8 Be sensitive to group members who do not have any children. They can participate in this question by sharing about a friend with whom they have had a "teachable moment."

Question 9 "In v. 34 three conditions are laid down which must be fulfilled by a loyal follower of Jesus. Two are decisive acts and the third is a continuous relationship. The first is self-denial. The second demand is to accept the last consequences of obedience, 'take up the cross,' 'a stake.,' 'the cross,' as an instrument of death. The third requirement is sustained loyalty in discipleship" (Vincent Taylor, *The Gospel According to Mark*, p. 381).

Question 10 "*Deny himself*. Cease to make self the object of his life and actions. *Take up his cross*. The picture of a man, already condemned, required to carry the beam of his own cross to the place of execution. Cross-bearing is a willingness to suffer and die for the Lord's sake. *And follow me*. Implying that his own death would be by crucifixion" (*The NIV Study Bible*, p. 1510).

NOTES